THE WORLD IS FULL OF SPIRITS

NATIVE AMERICAN RELIGION, MYTHOLOGY AND LEGENDS

US History for Kids

Children's American History

Long before Europeans "discovered" the New World, North America was filled with millions of people, members of hundreds of tribes and nations. What did they believe about how and why they were there? Let's find out!

A WORLD FULL OF PEOPLE AND SPIRITS

The many Native American tribes of North America had a wide range of beliefs and practices. But there were some beliefs that almost every tribe shared. Here are some:

Woman With Hawk Spirit

THE GREAT SPIRIT

Native Americans believed that while each person each animal, and every living thing is an individual, it is also connected to all other living things. That connection is through the Great Spirit, a creative force that gives us life and meaning. Some tribes called it the Great Mystery, the puzzle of life that we spend our lives trying to understand. The Great Spirit fills, and is the reason for, everything in the universe, from the stars down to drops of water.

THE IMPORTANCE OF ANIMALS

In the story of life for Native Americans, the animals are as filled with the Great Spirit as people are. Sometimes animals speak to people, guide them, or warn them. Some tribes understood a certain animal to be their special protector or "totem", giving members of that tribe special powers or ways of living in the world.

Many tribes thought that each individual animal was an image of the spirit of that species. Every fox was an image of the one Fox, and every bear of the one Bear.

THE FOUR DIRECTIONS

The Four Directions are points of balance in the Native American world view. They can be the points of the compass, four animals, or even four colors. Sometimes a fifth point of balance appears in the center of the Four Directions, like four brothers with their sister in the middle.

The Four Directions

MYTHS AND LEGENDS

◇◇◇◇◇◇◇◇◇◇◇◇◇◇◇◇◇◇◇◇◇◇◇◇◇◇

In the same way that the Greeks and Romans developed their myths to help them make sense of the world, Native Americans told and retold stories about the Great Spirit and the spirits working in people and animals.

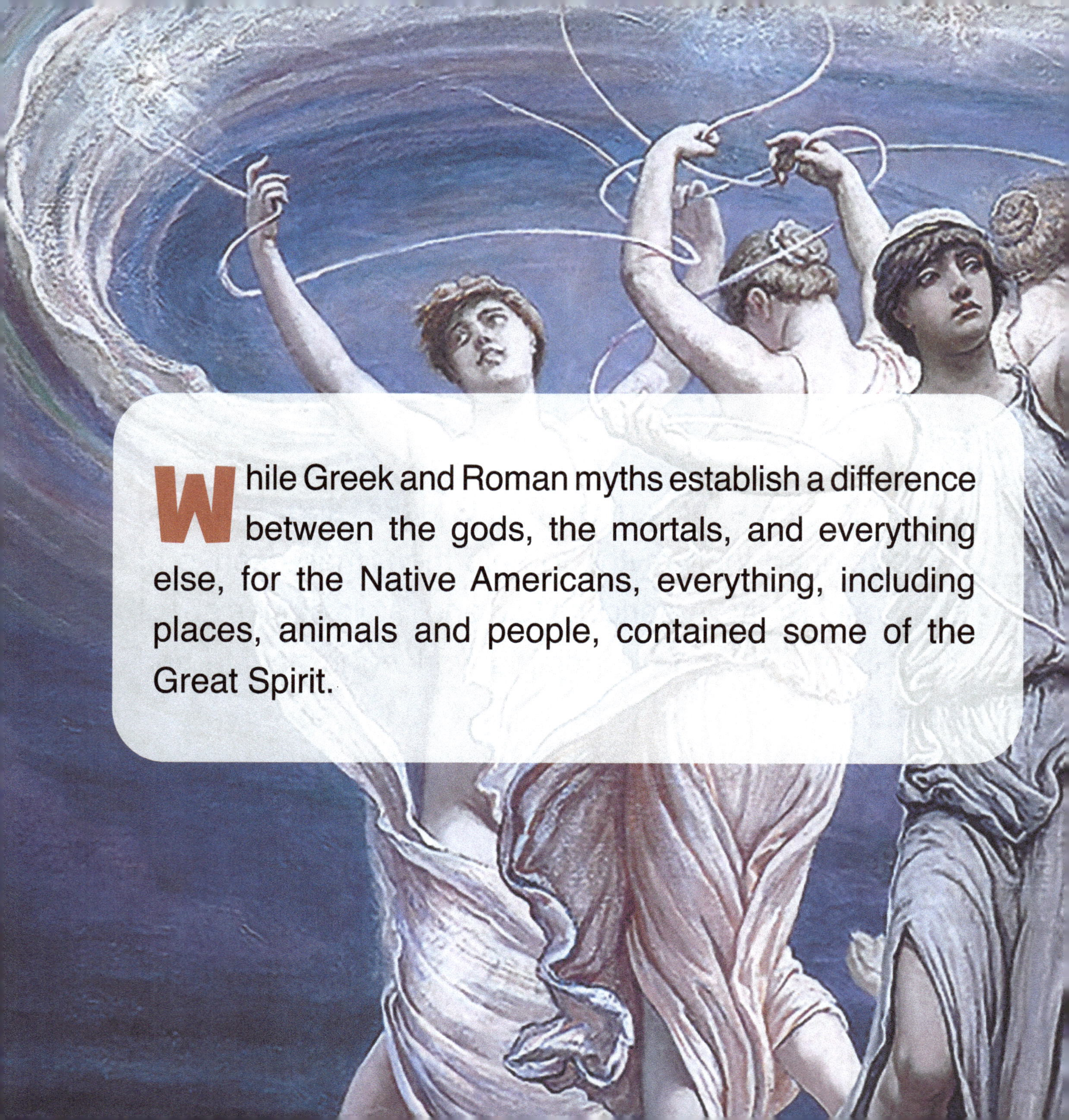

While Greek and Roman myths establish a difference between the gods, the mortals, and everything else, for the Native Americans, everything, including places, animals and people, contained some of the Great Spirit.

KING NEPTUNE GOD OF
THE SEA

In European myths, humans and gods have names and family connections; in North American myths and stories, the characters often have names that are just descriptions, like Rabbit Boy, First Woman, and Coyote.

Likes myths around the world, Native American myths and legends include common themes or "archetypes". Here are some:

- The hero who has to take a journey (Odysseus in the Greek myths; First Woman in the Native American myths)

- The orphan who becomes a great hero

- The wise old woman who helps the hero

- The trickster who must be defeated (Loki in the Norse myths; Coyote in some Native American myths)

THE FLOOD

Many Native American tribes shared a myth of a great flood. In most of the stories, a partly human creature sends a diving bird or a diving animal to get some mud or sand from under the sea to restore the land.

STAR-BORN

In many myths, the mother or father of the hero is a star, and then the hero comes to live on Earth and lead the people.

THE OLD MAN

Many tribes told long stories, with many episodes, of The Old Man, a magical human who could change his shape and who worked to right wrongs and defeat evil, but who also played tricks on people.

Among the Plains Indians and tribes on the Pacific Coast, the same stories appear about Coyote; and some tribes tell the stories about a spider called Unktomi.

WHITE BUFFALO WOMAN

The tribes of the Great Plains have as their central myth the story of how the people received the sacred peace pipe, and learned the ceremony of smoking it. In the myth, White Buffalo Woman appears to the people, gives them a bundle with a pipe and a sacred stone, explains the markings on the pipe and the stone and how and where to use them.

THE WHITE BUFFALO WOMAN

THE WHITE BUFFALO WOMAN

hen White Buffalo Woman walks around the teepee where the people are gathered, turns into a white buffalo, and leaves the people. When the people smoke the pipe together, they are also sharing it with the spirit world.

ANIMAL ORIGINS

Many myths try to explain how animals came to be as they are. In one Blackfoot myth, the trickster character is angry and tries to pull the lynx in half, but he only gives it a longer body.

THE GREAT SPIRIT IN ANIMALS

In many tales and myths, The Great Spirit, or the spirit of the prime animal (Coyote or Wolf, for instance) works through the specific coyote or wolf in the story to help the human characters in some way. In other stories the Great Spirit works through imaginary animals, as when Thunderbird (a creature like an eagle) makes lightning and thunder happen.

RELIGIOUS PRACTICES

Rituals and ceremonies are central to Native American traditional culture. For Native Americans, these practices are not something you choose to do, like choosing to go to church on Sunday. They are more like essential practices, the way you cannot see without opening your eyelids.

THE BLACKFOOT RITUAL

Native American rituals are closely related to how they traditionally gathered food, and give a way to celebrate and respond to important stages in life, like birth, coming of age, marriage, and death.

DEATH CEREMONIES

Native Americans believed that death in this world opened the way to life in the Spirit World. Many rituals were to help the dead person find the path and start on the journey. In rituals, people would offer the dead person the food, herbs, and other gifts needed on the journey.

avajo people believed that if a person died by accident, suicide, or sudden illness, instead of dying of old age, an evil spirit, a "Chindi" could cause trouble for the dead person's family. Rituals lasting several days tried to restore order in the family and in the Spirit World.

GREEN CORN FESTIVALS

People of the eastern woodlands and the southeastern part of North America held celebrations in the late summer to give thanks to the Great Spirit for corn, rain, sun, and the harvest. This is also a time for council meetings at which minor problems and even crimes that took place in the past year could be forgiven. This helped restore the spirit of the community.

HEALING RITUALS

Many different rituals tried to help restore harmony in a sick person, in a troubled family, or in a divided community. Tribes like the Navajo and Sioux would have ceremonies lasting several days, involving burning herbs, sacred dances, sand paintings, story telling, and times of silence.

PEYOTE WORSHIP

Tribes in the southwest have often performed ceremonies involving peyote (the fruit of a small cactus) or sacred mushrooms. The tea made from these materials could put the person who drank it into a sort of a waking dream, where the person could perceive reality differently and possibly hear a message from the Great Spirit or other spirits. The ceremonies also involved burning incense or herbs in a fire to help cleanse the mind, and wearing bird feathers to try to gather strength and vision from the bird spirits.

FLOWERING PEYOTE CACTUS

YOUNG KANZA WARRIOR FOND OF OLD TRADITIONS

VISION QUESTS

For many tribes, young men took a "vision quest" to try to find the direction of their lives. This was part of becoming an adult member of the tribe. The ritual and the quest varied from tribe to tribe, but usually involved a spiritual experience in which the young man tried to connect with a guardian spirit for advice or to gain strength.

The quests took a lot of preparation, and often included going into the wilderness and surviving without food or shelter for several days. This was to help the person become aware of the voices of the spirit world. For other tribes, the quest did not involve a physical journey. The

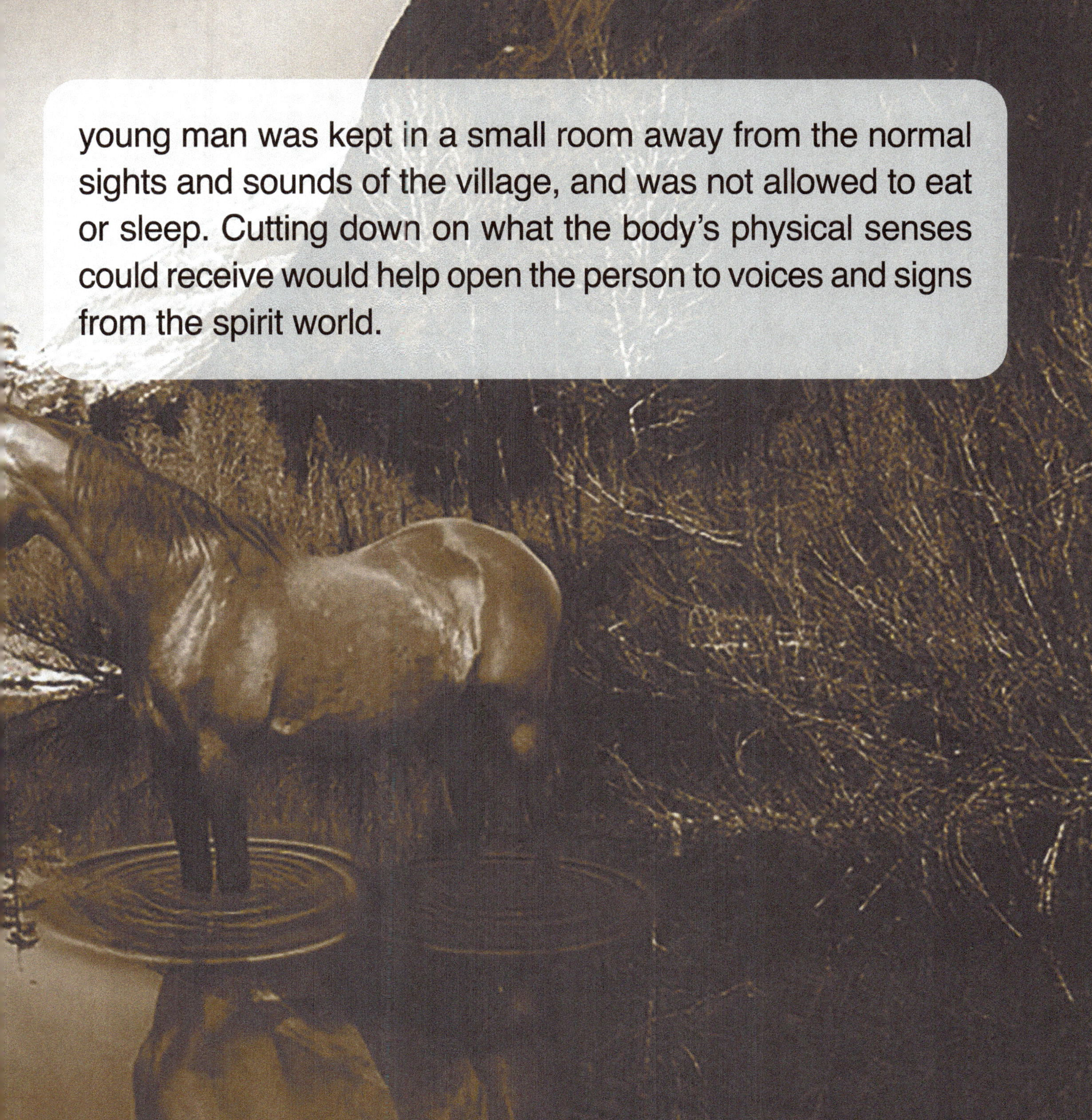

young man was kept in a small room away from the normal sights and sounds of the village, and was not allowed to eat or sleep. Cutting down on what the body's physical senses could receive would help open the person to voices and signs from the spirit world.

JHSHARP

After the young man completed the quest, he would return to the tribe, complete the rituals celebrating his becoming a full grown-up in the tribe, and pursue his life according to what he had learned from the spirits.

KEEPING AWARE OF THE GREAT SPIRIT

After the Europeans came to the New World, conquering the Native Americans and taking their land, the people of the tribes tried to keep strong through their traditions, stories, and spiritual practices.

PRAYER TO THE SPIRIT
OF THE BUFFALO

Native Americans suffered the violence of war, being forced out of their traditional territories and ways of life, and deaths of large numbers of their people from diseases the Europeans brought. It is amazing that so

many tribes still survive and are able to maintain some
of their culture and beliefs, even under heavy pressure
from the dominant culture of the newcomers.

Read other Baby Professor books, like King Philip's War and The Wounded Knee Massacre, to learn more about the Native American experience after the arrival of the Europeans.

Visit

BABY PROFESSOR
EDUCATION KIDS

www.BabyProfessorBooks.com

to download Free Baby Professor eBooks
and view our catalog of new and exciting
Children's Books